Thru the Bible
In 52 Weeks

Including a Brief Introduction to all
Sixty-Six Books of the Bible

Mel Hooten

To my Grandchildren & Great-Grandchildren

I dedicate this book with the prayer

That the Living Word of God may be as loved, read and

Believed in as it is by their Papa.

"Your word is a lamp to my feet and a light to path"—
Psalm. 119:105

Contents

Foreword

I've met lots of folks who say, "Someday, I am going to read through the Bible." In fact, I suspect that is the goal of most Christians. And there are many who actually get started, but somewhere along the way, maybe at the "begats . . ." in Genesis, they get bogged down, and give up. I know—I've been there too.

Thru the Bible in 52 Weeks is not a perfect plan, but it is different from all others that I have seen. For one thing, it starts at a different place than most other reading plans. *Thru the Bible in 52 Weeks* begins with the joyful book of Philippians and allows you to 'bounce' back-and-forth on an exciting journey between New and Old Testaments. It is not a straight path through the Bible as many plans are, but is a scenic tour that takes you month-by-month and week-by-week from history, to poetry, to prophecy, to a variegated view of the Bible.

Thru the Bible in 52 Weeks will systematically take you through the comfort and inspiration of the Psalms four times during the year. Every day you will reflect upon the words of poets like David who passed through the worst and best of life. And you will benefit immensely from the practical wisdom of King Solomon. God granted him great wisdom which included the ability to learn from his mistakes and pass that wisdom along to us through his books. You will read one-chapter-per-day from his Book of Proverbs. Taking to heart the Psalms and Proverbs every day can increase your faith and change the way you live. The person who lays the Bible down after consuming a daily dose of Psalms and Proverbs will not be the same as the one who picked it up one year before.

Each day of the year, you will open the pages of Psalms and Proverbs. You will then follow the plan through either a book from the Old Testament or the New. The more you read, the better you will be able to see a common thread that runs through the length of the pages of the Bible, that it is all about God's redemptive plan to save a lost humanity through the gift of His Son, Jesus Christ. This is made evident not just in Scriptures like John 3:16, but you will see it in places like Leviticus, Nehemiah, Isaiah, Daniel, Joel; in fact, anywhere you open the Bible, you will see it, the red cord of redemption.

Besides suggested Scripture readings, *Thru the Bible in 52 Weeks* also includes as brief description of each book of the Bible, all sixty-six of them. Each description includes the human author, purpose of the book, date of its writing, and a key verse and message. Each description is strategically placed to enable you know something about the Bible book before reading it.

Each day's reading from *Thru the Bible in 52 Weeks* will require something like 15 – 20 minutes. The reading plan can easily be divided into sections to be read at different times in the day. For example, you might want to read the Psalms and Proverbs early in the day and the suggested reading section from another Book of the Bible before turning in at night. However you choose to use this plan, my hope and prayer is that this is the time you'll not just get started, but that you will actually complete your plan to read through the Bible. And once you have done it, you'll want to do it again.

Let me know how it goes. Any thoughts, testimonies, questions, concerns, prayer needs—I will be excited to hear from you. mel.pardner@gmail.com.

Or visit my website www.CowboyCountryGospel.com

Psalms & Proverbs

Each and every day of the year, *Thru the Bible in 52 weeks* will take you to the inspiration and comfort of the Psalms and the wisdom of Proverbs. When one finds a copy of only the New Testament on a bookshelf, it will often include the Psalms and Proverbs of the Old Testament. At the onset of this plan, it is important that we take a look at the background of these two very significant books of the Bible.

Psalms

An Ancient Book of Inspirational Poetry

Writers of the Book of Psalms: Psalms is often referred to as "The Psalms of David." He is the author of at least 73 of the Psalms. Asaph wrote 12 of the psalms; the Sons of Korah wrote 9; Solomon wrote two and Moses is credited with one. Two "*Ezarahites*", Herman and Ethan wrote one each (Herman Psalm 88, and Ethan Psalm 89). About fifty-one of the psalms are anonymous.

Purpose of Psalms: To provide poetry for the expression of praise, worship and confession to God.

Date of the writing of the Psalms: Between 1490 (the time of Moses)-444 B.C. (days of Ezra, the scribe).

Key Verse: "Let everything that has breath praise the LORD. Praise the LORD!" (**Psalm 150:6**)

Key Message of Psalms: To Praise God.

Original Recipients of the Book of the Psalms: The People of Israel

Proverbs

A Book of Wisdom

Writers of Proverbs: King Solomon, Agur and Lemuel

Purpose of Proverbs: To help us to attain wisdom and discipline and to teach us to live a life that is right, just and fair. It has been called a "textbook for teaching people how to live godly lives through the repetition of wise thoughts."

Date of the writing of Proverbs: Approximately 970-930 B.C.

Key Verse: The fear of the LORD is the beginning of knowledge; Fools despise wisdom and instruction. (**Proverbs 1:7**)

Key Message: To live a life of wisdom.

Original Recipients of the Book of Proverbs: The People of Israel

Thru the Bible

In 52 Weeks

Including a Brief Introduction to all

Sixty-Six Books of the Bible

Philippians

A Letter of Joy

Writer of Philippians: The Apostle Paul

Purpose of Philippians: To thank the Church in Philippi for their gifts and to encourage them in their time of trials and suffering. Also, to warn them about false teachers.

Date of the writing of Philippians: Approximately A.D. 60-62 from Rome.

Key Verse in Philippians: "Rejoice in the Lord always; again, I will say, rejoice! (**Philippians 4:4**).

Key Message of Philippians: Joy

Original Recipients of the Letter of Philippians: The Church in Philippi

Colossians

The Fulness of Christ

Writer of Colossians: The Apostle Paul

Purpose of Colossians: To combat errors in the church and to show that born-again Christians have everything they need in Christ.

Date of the writing of Colossians: Around A.D. 61 during Paul's imprisonment in Rome.

Key Verses in Colossians: "For in Him all the fullness of Deity dwells in bodily form,
and in Him you have been made complete, and He is the head over all rule and authority" (**Colossians 2:9, 10**).

Key Theme of Colossians: Jesus Christ is Lord

Original Recipients of the Letter of Colossians: Churches in Colossi and Laodicea.

Jeremiah

A Prophetic Warning

Writer of Jeremiah: Jeremiah, often called the "Weeping Prophet".

Purpose of Jeremiah: To warn God's people of judgement and to urge them to repent and seek God's forgiveness before it was too late.

Date of the Writing of Jeremiah: Approximately 585 – 580 B.C.

Key Verse in Jeremiah: "'Your own wickedness will correct you, and your apostasies will reprove you; Know therefore and see that it is evil and bitter for you to forsake the LORD your God, and the dread of Me is not in you,' declares the Lord GOD of hosts" (**Jeremiah 2:19**).

Key Message in Jeremiah: God's people who will not repent of their sins will face severe consequences.

Original Recipients of the Book of Jeremiah: Judah (the southern kingdom) and the city of Jerusalem.

Week 1

Day 1
Psalms 1- 2
Proverbs 1
Philippians 1 – 2

Day 2
Psalms 3 – 4
Proverbs 2
Philippians 3 – 4

Day 3
Psalms 5 – 6
Proverbs 3
Colossians 1 – 2

Day 4
Psalms 7 - 8
Proverbs 4
Colossians 3 - 4

Day 5
Psalm 9
Proverbs 5
Jeremiah 1 - 3

Day 6
Psalms 10 – 11
Proverbs 6
Jeremiah 4 – 6

Day 7
Psalms 12 – 13
Proverbs 7
Jeremiah 7 - 10

Thoughts ~ Insights

_____
_____
_____
_____
_____
_____
_____
_____
_____
_____
_____

Week 2

Day 1
Psalms 14 – 15
Proverbs 8
Jeremiah 11 – 12

Day 2
Psalm 16
Proverbs 9
Jeremiah 13 – 15

Day 3
Psalm 17
Proverbs 10
Jeremiah 16 – 18

Day 4
Psalm 18
Proverbs 11
Jeremiah 19 – 20

Day 5
Psalms 19 – 20
Proverbs 12
Jeremiah 21 – 23

Day 6
Psalm 21
Proverbs 13
Jeremiah 24 – 26

Day 7
Psalm 22
Proverbs 14
Jeremiah 27 - 28

Thoughts ~ Insights

_____
_____
_____
_____
_____
_____
_____
_____
_____
_____
_____

Week 3

Day 1
  Psalms 23 – 24
  Proverbs 15
  Jeremiah 29 – 31

Day 2
  Psalms 25 – 26
  Proverbs 16
  Jeremiah 32 – 35

Day 3
  Psalms 27 – 28
  Proverbs 17
  Jeremiah 36 - 39

Day 4
  Psalms 29 – 30
  Proverbs 18
  Jeremiah 40 - 43

Day 5
  Psalms 31 – 32
  Proverbs 19
  Jeremiah 44 - 46

Day 6
  Psalms 33 – 34
  Proverbs 20
  Jeremiah 47 - 49

Day 7 Psalm 35
  Proverbs 21
  Jeremiah 50 - 52

Thoughts ~ Insights

_____
_____
_____
_____
_____
_____
_____
_____
_____
_____
_____

Lamentations
The Fall of a Kingdom

Writer of Lamentations: Jeremiah

Purpose of Lamentations: To warn God's people that to disobey Him is to invite His judgment. And to show that God suffers when His people suffer.

Date of the Writing of Lamentations: In 586 B.C. after the fall of Jerusalem

Key Verse in Lamentations: "My eyes fail because of tears, My spirit is greatly troubled; My heart is poured out on the earth because of the destruction of the daughter of My people, when little ones and infants faint in the streets of the city" (**Lamentations 2:11**).

Key Message in Lamentations: Severe Consequences of Sin

Original Recipients of Lamentations: The Southern Kingdom of Judah

Daniel
Faithfulness & Prophecy of Future Events

Writer of Daniel: Daniel

Purpose of Daniel: To encourage Jewish exiles during their Babylonian captivity and to remind them of God's ultimate victory and control over world events.

Date of the Writing of Daniel: Approximately from 536 – 530 B.C.

Key Verse in Daniel: "It is He who reveals the profound and hidden things; He knows what is in the darkness, and the light dwells with Him" **(Daniel 2:22)**.

Key Theme in Daniel: The Sovereignty of God
Original Recipients of the Book of Daniel: Jewish exiles in Babylon

I John
Fellowship with God

Writer of I John: John the Apostle

Purpose of I John: To expose false teachers and to give believers assurance of their salvation.

Date of the Writing of I John: Likely between the years of A.D. 85 – 90.

Key Verse in I John: "These things I have written to you who believe in the name of the Son of God, so that you may know that you have eternal life." **(I John 5:13)**.

Key Message in I John: Assurance of Salvation

Original Recipients of the Letter of I John: The letter was untitled and was sent as a Pastoral Letter to several congregations.

Week 4

Day 1
Psalms 36 – 37
Proverbs 22
Lamentations 1 – 5

Day 2
Psalms 38 – 39
Proverbs 23
Daniel 1 – 3

Day 3
Psalms 40 – 41
Proverbs 24
Daniel 4 – 6

Day 4
Psalms 42 – 43
Proverbs 25
Daniel 7 – 9

Day 5
Psalms 44
Proverbs 26
Daniel 10 – 12

Day 6
Psalm 45 - 46
Proverbs 27
I John 1 – 3

Day 7
Psalm 47 - 48
Proverbs 28
I John 4 - 5

Thoughts ~ Insights

_____
_____
_____
_____
_____
_____
_____
_____
_____
_____
_____

I Samuel
Transition

Writer of I Samuel: Probably Samuel, but also includes writings of the prophets, Nathan and Gad (**I Chronicles 29:29**) "Now the acts of King David, from first to last, are written in the chronicles of Samuel the seer, in the chronicles of Nathan the prophet and in the chronicles of Gad the seer."

Purpose of I Samuel: To record the life of Samuel, Israel's last judge and the transition from a theocracy to a monarchy in the Nation of Israel.

Date of the Writing of I Samuel: About 925 B.C.

Key Verses in I Samuel: "The LORD said to Samuel, 'Listen to the voice of the people in regard to all that they say to you, for they have not rejected you, but they have rejected Me from being king over them. . . Now then, listen to their voice; however, you shall solemnly warn them and tell them of the procedure of the king who will reign over them'" (**I Samuel 8: 7, 9**).

Key Message of I Samuel: A Nation in Transition to a Monarchy

Original Recipients of I Samuel: The people of Israel

Week 5

Day 1
Psalm 49
Proverbs 29
I Samuel 1 – 3

Day 2
Psalm 50
Proverbs 30
I Samuel 4 – 6

Day 3
Psalms 51 – 52
Proverbs 31
I Samuel 7 – 9

Day 4
Psalms 53 – 54
Proverbs 1
I Samuel 10 – 12

Day 5
Psalm 55
Proverbs 2
I Samuel 13 -14

Day 6
Psalms 56 – 57
Proverbs 3
I Samuel 15 – 16

Day 7
Psalms 58 – 59
Proverbs 4
I Samuel 17 - 19

Thoughts ~ Insights

_____
_____
_____
_____
_____
_____
_____
_____
_____
_____
_____

II Samuel
The Life and Times of King David

Writer of II Samuel: Unknown. It does however contain writings of the prophets, Nathan and Gad (**I Chronicles 29:29**).

Purpose of II Samuel: To record Israel's history from Saul's death to the end of David's reign.

Date of the writing of II Samuel: Around 930 B.C., soon after Kling David's death.

Key Verse: "And David realized that the LORD had established him as king over Israel, and that He had exalted his kingdom for the sake of His people Israel" (**II Samuel 5:12**).

Key Person in II Samuel: King David
Original Recipients of II Samuel: The people of Israel

Week 6

Day 1
  Psalms 60 – 61
  Proverbs 5
  I Samuel 20 – 22

Day 2
  Psalms 62 – 63
  Proverbs 6
  I Samuel 23 – 25

Day 3
  Psalms 64 – 65
  Proverbs 7
  I Samuel 26 – 28

Day 4
  Psalms 66 – 67
  Proverbs 8
  I Samuel 29 – 31

Day 5
  Psalm 68
  Proverbs 9
  II Samuel 1 – 2

Day 6
  Psalm 69
  Proverbs 10
  II Samuel 3 – 5

Day 7
  Psalms 70 – 72
  Proverbs 11
  II Samuel 6 - 9

Thoughts ~ Insights

_____
_____
_____
_____
_____
_____
_____
_____
_____
_____
_____

I Timothy
Pastoral Advice for a Young Preacher

Writer of I Timothy: The Apostle Paul

Purpose of I Timothy: To give encouragement and instruction to a young minister of the Gospel and to warn him about false teachers.

Date of the Writing of I Timothy: About A.D. 64, possibly from Rome just prior to Paul's final imprisonment in Rome.

Key Verse in I Timothy: "Let no one look down on your youthfulness, but *rather* in speech, conduct, love, faith *and* purity, show yourself an example of those who believe" (**I Timothy 4:12**).

Key Message of I Timothy: Encouragement for a young pastor in a tough situation.

Original Recipient of I Timothy: Timothy

Week 7

Day 1
Psalms 73 – 74
Proverbs 12
II Samuel 10 – 12

Day 2
Psalms 75 – 76
Proverbs 13
II Samuel 13 – 15

Day 3
Psalm 77
Proverbs 14
II Samuel 16 – 18

Day 4
Psalm 78
Proverbs 15
II Samuel 19 – 21

Day 5
Psalms 79 – 80
Proverbs 16
II Samuel 22 – 24

Day 6
Psalms 81 – 82
Proverbs 17
I Timothy 1 – 3

Day 7
Psalms 83 – 84
Proverbs 18
I Timothy 4 - 6

Thoughts ~ Insights

_____
_____
_____
_____
_____
_____
_____
_____
_____
_____
_____

II Timothy
An Apostle's Final Words

Writer of II Timothy: The Apostle Paul

Purpose of II Timothy: To give final instructions to this young pastor of the Church in Ephesus and to charge him to stay true to the pure Word of God.

Date of the Writing of II Timothy: A.D. 66 or 67 from a dungeon in Rome. Paul was executed under the Roman emperor Nero.

Key Verse in II Timothy: "Be diligent to present yourself approved to God as a workman who does not need to be ashamed, accurately handling the word of truth" (**II Timothy 2:15**).

Key Message of II Timothy: Paul's final words from a dungeon in Rome, written to encourage and to exhort a young pastor.

Original Recipient of II Timothy: Timothy

Amos
A Country Prophet

Writer of Amos: Amos

Purpose of Amos: To pronounce God's judgement on the Northern Kingdom of Israel for their sins of idolatry, immorality, complacency and oppression of the poor.

Date of the Writing of Amos: About 760 – 750 B.C. Probably during the reigns of Jeroboam II, King of Israel and Uzziah, King of Judah.

Key Verse in Amos: "But let justice roll down like waters and righteousness like an ever-flowing stream" (**Amos 5:24**).

Key Message of Amos: God's Righteousness and His Justice— "Prepare to meet your God, O Israel" (**Amos 4:12**).

Original Recipient of Amos: The People of Israel, the Northern Kingdom

ಎ∞ళ

Micah
Prophet to the Oppressed

Writer of Micah: Micah

Purpose of Micah: To warn God's people of approaching judgment and to offer pardon and forgiveness to all who repent.

Date of the Writing of Micah: Around 740 – 687 B.C. Possibly during the reigns of Jotham, Ahaz and Hezekiah, kings of the Southern Kingdom of Judah.

Key Verse in Micah: "He has told you, O man, what is good; And what does the LORD require of you but to do justice, to love kindness, and to walk humbly with your God? (**Micah 6:8**).

Key Message in Micah: Judgment and deliverance by God.

Original Recipients of Micah: The people of Israel, the Northern Kingdom and the people of Judah, the Southern Kingdom.

Week 8

Day 1
   Psalms 85 – 86
   Proverbs 19
   II Timothy 1 – 4

Day 2
   Psalms 87 – 88
   Proverbs 20
   Amos 1 – 3

Day 3
   Psalms 89
   Proverbs 21
   Amos 4 – 5

Day 4
   Psalms 90 - 92
   Proverbs 22
   Amos 6 – 9

Day 5
   Psalms 93 - 94
   Proverbs 23
   Micah 1 – 2

Day 6
   Psalms 95 – 96
   Proverbs 24
   Micah 3 – 4

Day 7
   Psalms 97 – 98
   Proverbs 25
   Micah 5 – 7

Thoughts ~ Insights

_____
_____
_____
_____
_____
_____
_____
_____
_____
_____

Revelation
An Unveiling of God's Truth and His Perfect Plan

Writer of Revelation: The Apostle John

Purpose of Revelation: To warn against falling away from the faith and the promise of final victory for all believers.

Date of the Writing of Revelation: Approximately A.D. 95 from the Island of Patmos where John was in exile.

Key Verse in Revelation: "Therefore write the things which you have seen, and the things which are, and the things which will take place after these things" (**Revelation 1:19**).

Key Message in Revelation: Jesus Christ is King of Kings and Lord of Lords; the First and the Last. All victory belongs to Him.

Original Recipients of Revelation: The seven churches in Asia (Revelation 2 & 3) and all believers everywhere.

Week 9

Day 1
Psalms 99 – 101
Proverbs 26
Revelation 1 – 3

Day 2
Psalms 102 – 103
Proverbs 27
Revelation 4 – 6

Day 3
Psalm 104
Proverbs 28
Revelation 7 – 10

Day 4
Psalm 105
Proverbs 29
Revelation 11 – 13

Day 5
Psalm 106
Proverbs 30
Revelation 14 – 16

Day 6
Psalm 107
Proverbs 31
Revelation 17 – 19

Day 7
Psalms 108 – 109
Proverbs 1
Revelation 20 - 22

Thoughts ~ Insights

_____
_____
_____
_____
_____
_____
_____
_____
_____
_____

Deuteronomy
Back to the Basics

Writer of Deuteronomy: Moses

Purpose of Deuteronomy: To remind God's people of what He had already done for them and to repeat again God's covenant and His commandments as they prepared to make transition into a new land and a new life.

Date of the Writing of Deuteronomy: About 1406 B.C.

Key Verse in Deuteronomy: "Know therefore that the LORD your God, He is God, the faithful God, who keeps His covenant and His lovingkindness to a thousandth generation with those who love Him and keep His commandments" (**Deuteronomy 7:9**).

Key Message in Deuteronomy: God's people are to devote themselves to Him wholeheartedly.

Original Recipients of Deuteronomy: The Children of Israel (the new generation entering the Promised Land).

Week 10

Day 1
Psalms 110 – 111
Proverbs 2
Deuteronomy 1 – 3

Day 2
Psalms 112 – 113
Proverbs 3
Deuteronomy 4 – 6

Day 3
Psalms 114 – 115
Proverbs 4
Deuteronomy 7 – 9

Day 4
Psalms 116 – 117
Proverbs 5
Deuteronomy 10 – 12

Day 5
Psalm 118
Proverbs 6
Deuteronomy 13 – 15

Day 6
Psalms 119:1 – 48
Proverbs 7
Deuteronomy 16 – 18

Day 7
Psalms 119:49 – 88
Proverbs 8
Deuteronomy 19 – 22

Thoughts ~ Insights

_____
_____
_____
_____
_____
_____
_____
_____
_____
_____

Ezra
Reformation

Writer of Ezra: Ezra

Purpose of Ezra: To show God's faithfulness in the restoring of land to the returning exiles from captivity.

Date of the Writing of Ezra: Around 440 B.C.

Key Verses in Ezra: "For Ezra had set his heart to study the law of the LORD and to practice *it,* and to teach *His* statutes and ordinances in Israel.

Key Message in Ezra: Reformation and Revival

Original Recipients of Ezra: The Exiles who had Returned Home from Captivity.

ॐॐ

Week 11

Day 1
Psalm 119:98 – 128
Proverbs 9
Deuteronomy 23 – 25

Day 2
Psalm 119:129 – 176
Proverbs 10
Deuteronomy 26 – 28

Day 3
Psalms 120 – 121
Proverbs 11
Deuteronomy 29 – 31

Day 4
Psalm 122
Proverbs 12
Deuteronomy 32 – 34

Day 5
Psalms 123 – 124
Proverbs 13
Ezra 1 – 3

Day 6
Psalms 125 – 126
Proverbs 14
Ezra 4 – 6

Day 7
Psalms 127 – 128
Proverbs 15
Ezra 7 - 10

Thoughts ~ Insights

_____
_____
_____
_____
_____
_____
_____
_____
_____
_____

John
The Gospel that Helps us Believe

Writer of the Gospel of John: John the Apostle

Purpose of John's Gospel: To conclusively prove that Jesus is the Son of God and that all who believe in Him will have eternal life.

Date of the Writing of John: Likely A.D. 85 – 90

Key verses in John: "Therefore many other signs Jesus also performed in the presence of the disciples, which are not written in this book; but these have been written so that you may believe that Jesus is the Christ, the Son of God; and that believing you may have life in His name" (**John 20:30-31**).

Key Message in John: Jesus is the Christ, the Son of God.

Original Recipients of John's Gospel: Christians and Searching non-Christians

Week 12

Day 1
Psalms 129 – 130
Proverbs 16
John 1 – 3

Day 2
Psalms 131 -132
Proverbs 17
John 4 – 6

Day 3
Psalms 133 – 134
Proverbs 18
John 7 – 8

Day 4
Psalm 135
Proverbs 19
John 9 – 10

Day 5
Psalms 136 – 137
Proverbs 20
John 11 – 12

Day 6   Psalm 138
Proverbs 21
John 13 – 14

Day 7
Psalms 139
Proverbs 22
John 15 - 16

Thoughts ~ Insights

_____
_____
_____
_____
_____
_____
_____
_____
_____
_____
_____

Ruth
A Love Story

Writer of Ruth: Unknown

Purpose of Ruth: To show how three people (Naomi, Ruth and Boaz) remained true to God even in the midst of sinful and challenging times. And also, to trace the generations and heritage of King David (**Ruth 4:18-22**).

Date of the Writing of Ruth: Probably around 1000 B.C.

Key Verse in Ruth: "But Ruth said, 'Do not urge me to leave you *or* turn back from following you; for where you go, I will go, and where you lodge, I will lodge. Your people *shall be* my people, and your God, my God'" (**Ruth 1:16**).

Key Message in Ruth: God is with us in difficult times; He does not abandon us.

Original Recipients of Ruth: The People of Israel

Obadiah
God's Judgment Against the Proud and Arrogant

Writer of Obadiah: Obadiah. Little is known of Obadiah; His name means "Servant" or "Worshiper" of the Lord.

Purpose of Obadiah: To condemn the arrogance of the Edomites and to pronounce judgment on them.

Date of the Writing of Obadiah: About 853 – 841 B.C.

Key Verse in Obadiah: "'Though you build high like the eagle, Though you set your nest among the stars, From there I will bring you down,' declares the Lord" (**Verse 4**).

Key Message in Obadiah: Unchecked Pride and Revenge will ultimately lead to Judgment and condemnation.

Original Recipients of Obadiah: The Edomites and the Jews in the Southern Kingdom of Judah.

Philemon
Grace and Forgiveness

Writer of Philemon: Apostle Paul

Purpose of Philemon: To appeal to Philemon to forgive Onesimus, his run-away slave and receive him back as a brother in Christ.

Date of the Writing of Philemon: Approximately A.D. 60 – 62 During Paul's Imprisonment in Rome.

Key Verses in Philemon: "For perhaps he was separated from you for a while, that you would have him back forever, no longer as a slave, but more than a slave, a beloved brother, especially to me, but how much more to you, both in the flesh and in the Lord" (**Verse 15-16**).

Key Message in Philemon: To forgive one by whom you have been wronged.

Original Recipient of Philemon: Philemon who may have been a member of the Colossian Church.

Zephaniah
Prophet with a Royal Heritage

Writer of Zephaniah: The Prophet Zephaniah

Purpose of Zephaniah: To urge the people of Judah to repent and turn back to God.

Date of the Writing of Zephaniah: Around 640-630 B.C.

Key Verse in Zephaniah: "Near is the great day of the LORD, Near and coming very quickly; Listen, the day of the LORD! In it the warrior cries out bitterly" **(Zephaniah 1:14)**.

Key Message in Zephaniah: Repentance; Return to God

Original Recipients of Zephaniah: People of the Southern Kingdom of Judah

Joshua
Faith is the Victory

Writer of Joshua: Joshua, except for the ending which may have been written by Phineas the High Priest who was an eye-witness to the events.

Purpose of Joshua: To record the historical events of the entry, conquest and division of the Promised Land.

Date of the Writing of Joshua: Approximately 1390 B.C.

Key Verse in Joshua: "Pass through the midst of the camp and command the people, saying, 'Prepare provisions for yourselves, for within three days you are to cross this Jordan, to go in to possess the land which the LORD your God is giving you, to possess it'" **(Joshua 1:11)**.

Key Message in Joshua: Faith in a Faithful God

Original Recipients of Joshua: The people of Israel

Week 13

Day 1
   Psalms 140 – 141
   Proverbs 23
   John 17 – 18

Day 2
   Psalms 142 – 143
   Proverbs 24
   John 19 – 21

Day 3
   Psalm 144
   Proverbs 25
   Ruth 1 – 2

Day 4
   Psalms 145 – 146
   Proverbs 26
   Ruth 3 – 4

Day 5
   Psalm 147
   Proverbs 27
   Obadiah & Philemon

Day 6
   Psalms 148 – 149
   Proverbs 28
   Zephaniah 1 – 3

Day 7   Psalm 150
   Proverbs 29
   Joshua 1 – 3

Thoughts ~ Insights

_____
_____
_____
_____
_____
_____
_____
_____
_____

Week 14

Day 1
Psalms 1 – 2
Proverbs 30
Joshua 4 – 8

Day 2
Psalms 3 – 4
Proverbs 31
Joshua 9 – 11

Day 3
Psalms 5 – 6
Proverbs 1
Joshua 12 – 14

Day 4
Psalms 7 – 8
Proverbs 2
Joshua 15 – 17

Day 5
Psalm 9
Proverbs 3
Joshua 18 – 20

Day 6
Psalms 10 – 11
Proverbs 4
Joshua 21 – 22

Day 7
Psalms 12 – 13
Proverbs 5
Joshua 23 – 24

Thoughts ~ Insights

_____
_____
_____
_____
_____
_____
_____
_____
_____
_____

I Corinthians
Church Conflict

Writer of I Corinthians: The Apostle Paul

Purpose of I Corinthians: To identify problems in the Corinthian church, to instruct the believers in proper Christian conduct and worship, and to deal with strife and division in the church.

Date of the Writing of I Corinthians: A.D. 54 – 55

Key Verse in I Corinthians: "Now I exhort you, brethren, by the name of our Lord Jesus Christ, that you all agree and that there be no divisions among you, but that you be made complete in the same mind and in the same judgment" (**I Corinthians 1:10**).

Key Message in I Corinthians: To deal with some un-Christian behavior in the Church.

Original Recipients of I Corinthians: The Church in Corinth

Nahum
Consequences of a Negligent Generation

Writer of Nahum: The Prophet Nahum

Purpose of Nahum: To pronounce God's judgment on the nation of Assyria and to assure God's people that evil does not endure forever.

Date of the Writing of Nahum: Around 663 – 609 B.C.

Key Verses in Nahum: "The LORD is good, A stronghold in the day of trouble, And He knows those who take refuge in Him. But with an overflowing flood He will make a complete end of its site (*NIV, Nineveh*), And will pursue His enemies into darkness. Whatever you devise against the LORD, He will make a complete end of it. Distress will not rise up twice" (**Nahum 1:7-9**).

Key Message in Nahum: The impending destruction of Nineveh, the capital city of Assyria.

Original Recipients of Nahum: The people of Nineveh and the people of the Southern Kingdom of Judah.

Week 15

Day 1
Psalms 14 – 15
Proverbs 6
I Corinthians 1 – 3

Day 2
Psalm 16
Proverbs 7
I Corinthians 4 – 6

Day 3
Psalm 17
Proverbs 8
I Corinthians 7 – 9

Day 4
Psalm 18
Proverbs 9
I Corinthians 10 – 12

Day 5
Psalms 19 – 20
Proverbs 10
I Corinthians 13 – 14

Day 6
Psalm 21
Proverbs 11
I Corinthians 15 – 16

Day 7
Psalm 22
Proverbs 12
Nahum 1 – 3

Thoughts ~ Insights

_____
_____
_____
_____
_____
_____
_____
_____
_____
_____

Ecclesiastes
Without God, All is Meaningless

Writer of Ecclesiastes: Solomon

Purpose of Ecclesiastes: To spare future generations from the bitter experience that life apart from God is meaningless.

Date of the Writing of Ecclesiastes: Likely 930 – 935 B.C.

Key Verses in Ecclesiastes: "Thus I considered all my activities which my hands had done and the labor which I had exerted, and behold all was vanity and striving after wind and there was no profit under the sun" (**Ecclesiastes 2:11**).

"The conclusion, when all has been heard, *is:* fear God and keep His commandments, because this *applies to* every person" (**Ecclesiastes 12:13**).

Key Message in Ecclesiastes: Life apart from God is empty and meaningless.

Original Recipients of Ecclesiastes: King Solomon's subjects in particular and all people in general.

Romans
Letter of Christian Doctrine

Writer of Romans: Apostle Paul

Purpose of Romans: To prepare for Paul's upcoming trip to Rome by way of an introduction and to present the basic doctrines of the Christian faith.

Date of the Writing of Romans: Winter of A.D. 57 from the city of Corinth.

Key Verses in Romans: "I am under obligation both to Greeks and to barbarians, both to the wise and to the foolish. So, for my part, I am eager to preach the gospel to you also who are in Rome. For I am not ashamed of the gospel, for it is the power of God for salvation to everyone who believes, to the Jew first and also to the Greek. For in it *the* righteousness of God is revealed from faith to faith; as it is written, "BUT THE RIGHTEOUS *man* SHALL LIVE BY FAITH" (**Romans 1:14-17**).

Key Message in Romans: Justified by faith

Original Recipients of Romans: The Christians in Rome

Day 1
  Psalms 23 – 24
  Proverbs 13
  Ecclesiastes 1 – 3

Day 2
  Psalms 25 – 26
  Proverbs 14
  Ecclesiastes 4 – 6

Day 3
  Psalms 27 – 28
  Proverbs 15
  Ecclesiastes 7 – 9

Day 4
  Psalms 29 – 30
  Proverbs 16
  Ecclesiastes 10 – 12

Day 5
  Psalms 31 - 32
  Proverbs 17
  Romans 1 – 3

Day 6
  Psalms 33 – 34
  Proverbs 18
  Romans 4 – 6

Day 7 Psalm 35
  Proverbs 19
  Romans 7 – 8

Thoughts ~ Insights

_____

_____

_____

_____

_____

_____

_____

_____

_____

_____

Numbers
Wilderness Wanderings

Writer of Numbers: Moses

Purpose of Numbers: To tell the story of Israel preparing to enter the Promised Land, how they rebelled, the resulting consequences of their rebellion and of their preparation to enter again.

Date of the Writing of Numbers: Likely around 1410 – 1406 B.C.

Key Verse in Numbers: "Surely all the men who have seen My glory and My signs which I performed in Egypt and in the wilderness, yet have put Me to the test these ten times and have not listened to My voice, shall by no means see the land which I swore to their fathers, nor shall any of those who spurned Me see it" (**Numbers 14:22-23**).

Key Message in Numbers: God is faithful to keep His promise even when His people are not.

Original Recipients of Numbers: The People of Israel

Week 17

Day 1
Psalms 36 – 37
Proverbs 20
Romans 9 – 10

Day 2
Psalms 38 – 39
Proverbs 21
Romans 11 – 13

Day 3
Psalms 40 – 41
Proverbs 22
Romans 14 – 16

Day 4
Psalms 42 – 43
Proverbs 23
Numbers 1 – 4

Day 5
Psalm 44
Proverbs 24
Numbers 5 – 7

Day 6
Psalms 45 – 46
Proverbs 25
Numbers 8 – 9

Day 7
Psalms 47 – 48
Proverbs 26
Numbers 10 – 11

Thoughts ~ Insights

_____
_____
_____
_____
_____
_____
_____
_____
_____
_____

Week 18

Day 1
Psalm 49
Proverbs 27
Numbers 12 – 13

Day 2
Psalm 50
Proverbs 28
Numbers 14 – 17

Day 3
Psalms 51 – 52
Proverbs 29
Numbers 18 – 20

Day 4
Psalms 53 – 54
Proverbs 30
Numbers 21 – 23

Day 5
Psalm 55
Proverbs 31
Numbers 24 – 27

Day 6
Psalms 56 – 57
Proverbs 1
Numbers 28 – 30

Day 7
Psalms 58 – 59
Proverbs 2
Numbers 31 – 33

Thoughts ~ Insights

_____
_____
_____
_____
_____
_____
_____
_____
_____
_____

Luke
A Physician's Account

Writer of Luke: Luke

Purpose of Luke: To give an accurate and detailed account of the life of Jesus and to present Him as the perfect human and Savior.

Date of the Writing of Luke: About A.D. 60

Key Verses in Luke: "And Jesus said to him, 'Today salvation has come to this house, because he, too, is a son of Abraham. For the Son of Man has come to seek and to save that which was lost'" (**Luke 19:9-10**).

Key Message in Luke's Gospel: Jesus is truly human

Original Recipients of Luke: Theophilus and Gentiles

Week 19

Day 1
  Psalms 60 – 61
  Proverbs 3
  Numbers 34 – 36

Day 2
  Psalms 62 – 63
  Proverbs 4
  Luke 1 – 2

Day 3
  Psalms 64 – 65
  Proverbs 5
  Luke 3 – 5

Day 4
  Psalms 66 – 67
  Proverbs 6
  Luke 6 – 7

Day 5
  Psalm 68
  Proverbs 7
  Luke 8 – 9

Day 6
  Psalm 69
  Proverbs 8
  Luke 10 -11

Day 7
  Psalms 70 – 71
  Proverbs 9
  Luke 12 – 14

Thoughts ~ Insights

_____
_____
_____
_____
_____
_____
_____
_____
_____

Zechariah
Prophet with a Vision

Writer of Zechariah: The Prophet Zechariah

Purpose of Zechariah: To encourage and give hope to God's people by revealing to them the promise of God's future deliverance through the coming Messiah.

Date of the Writing of Zechariah: Around 520 B.C.

Key Verses in Zechariah: "Rejoice greatly, O daughter of Zion! Shout *in triumph,* O daughter of Jerusalem! Behold, your king is coming to you; He is just and endowed with salvation, humble, and mounted on a donkey, even on a colt, the foal of a donkey. I will cut off the chariot from Ephraim and the horse from Jerusalem; and the bow of war will be cut off. And He will speak peace to the nations; and His dominion will be from sea to sea, and from the River to the ends of the earth" (**Zechariah 9:9-10**).

Key Message in Zechariah: Encouragement, motivation and hope for God's people—promise of the coming Messiah.

Original Recipients of Zechariah: The Jews in Jerusalem who had returned from captivity.

Week 20

Day 1
Psalms 73 – 74
Proverbs 10
Luke 15 – 16

Day 2
Psalms 75 – 76
Proverbs 11
Luke 17 – 19

Day 3
Psalm 77
Proverbs 12
Luke 20 – 22

Day 4
Psalm 78
Proverbs 13
Luke 23 – 24

Day 5
Psalms 79 – 80
Proverbs 14
Zechariah 1 – 4

Day 6
Psalms 81 – 82
Proverbs 15
Zechariah 5 – 8

Day 7
Psalms 83 – 84
Proverbs 16
Zechariah 9 – 11

Thoughts ~ Insights
_____
_____
_____
_____
_____
_____
_____
_____
_____
_____

Judges
The Dark Ages

Writer of Judges: Unknown; possibly Samuel

Purpose of Judges: To show God's love and forgiveness when man's behavior is at its worst.

Date of the writing of Judges: Likely around 1000 B.C.

Key Verse in Judges: "In those days there was no king in Israel; everyone did what was right in his own eyes" (**Judges 21:25**).

Key Message in Judges: To record Israel's history during the period of the Judges; a spiritually dark time in Israel's history when "everyone did what was right in his own eyes."

Original Recipients of Judges: The people of Israel

Week 21

Day 1
  Psalms 85 – 86
  Proverbs 17
  Zechariah 9 – 11

Day 2
  Psalms 87 – 88
  Proverbs 18
  Zechariah 12 – 14

Day 3
  Psalm 89
  Proverbs 19
  Judges 1 – 3

Day 4
  Psalms 90 – 92
  Proverbs 20
  Judges 4 – 6

Day 5
  Psalms 93 – 94
  Proverbs 21
  Judges 7 – 9

Day 6
  Psalms 95 – 96
  Proverbs 22
  Judges 10 – 12

Day 7
  Psalms 97 – 98
  Proverbs 23
  Judges 13 – 14

Thoughts ~ Insights

_____
_____
_____
_____
_____
_____
_____
_____
_____
_____

Ephesians
The Body of Christ

Writer of Ephesians: The Apostle Paul

Purpose of Ephesians: To encourage and strengthen Christians in Ephesus by helping them understand the nature and purpose of the church, the Body of Christ.

Date of the Writing of Ephesians: Around A.D. 60 from Rome during Paul's imprisonment.

Key Verses in Ephesians: "*There is* one body and one Spirit, just as also you were called in one hope of your calling; one Lord, one faith, one baptism, one God and Father of all who is over all and through all and in all" (**Ephesians 4:4-6**).

Key Message in Ephesians: Through redemption, we are all made one in the Body of Christ.

Original Recipients of Ephesians: Sent to the Church in Ephesus and then as a circulating letter to other churches.

I Kings
Solomon and a Kingdom Divided

Writer of I Kings: Unknown

Purpose of I Kings: To describe the process of going from a united to a divided kingdom.

Date of the Writing of I Kings: Probably 560-550 B.C.

Key Verses in I Kings: "As for you, if you will walk before Me as your father David walked, in integrity of heart and uprightness, doing according to all that I have commanded you *and* will keep My statutes and My ordinances, then I will establish the throne of your kingdom over Israel forever, just as I promised to your father David, saying, 'You shall not lack a man on the throne of Israel'" (**I Kings 9:4-5**).

Key Message of I Kings: A divided kingdom

Original Recipients of I Kings: The People of Israel

Week 22

Day 1
  Psalms 99 – 101
  Proverbs 24
  Judges 15 – 17

Day 2
  Psalms 102 – 103
  Proverbs 25
  Judges 18 – 21

Day 3
  Psalm 104
  Proverbs 26
  Ephesians 1 – 2

Day 4
  Psalm 105
  Proverbs 27
  Ephesians 3 - 4

Day 5
  Psalm 106
  Proverbs 28
  Ephesians 5 – 6

Day 6
  Psalm 107
  Proverbs 29
  I Kings 1 – 4

Day 7
  Psalms 108 – 109
  Proverbs 30
  I Kings 5 - 8

Thoughts ~ Insights

_____
_____
_____
_____
_____
_____
_____
_____
_____
_____

II Kings
Road to Captivity

Writer of II Kings: Unknown

Purpose of II Kings: To record the sinful rebellion and downfall of the kingdoms of Israel and Judah.

Date of the Writing of II Kings: Likely 560-550 B.C.

Key Verse in II Kings: "Yet the LORD warned Israel and Judah through all His prophets *and* every seer, saying, 'Turn from your evil ways and keep My commandments, My statutes according to all the law which I commanded your fathers, and which I sent to you through My servants the prophets.' However, they did not listen, but stiffened their neck like their fathers, who did not believe in the LORD their God" (**II Kings 17:13-14**).

Key Message in II Kings: Willfully sinning against God can be forgiven, but the brutal consequences cannot be erased.

Original Recipients of II Kings: The People of Israel

Week 23

Day 1
  Psalms 110 – 111
  Proverbs 31
  I Kings 9 - 13

Day 2
  Psalms 112 – 113
  Proverbs 1
  I Kings 14 - 18

Day 3
  Psalms 114 – 115
  Proverbs 2
  I Kings 19 - 22

Day 4
  Psalms 116 – 117
  Proverbs 3
  II Kings 1 – 4

Day 5
  Psalms 118
  Proverbs 4
  II Kings 5 – 8

Day 6
  Psalm 119:1 – 48
  Proverbs 5
  II Kings 9 – 12

Day 7
  Psalm119:49 – 88
  Proverbs 6
  II Kings 13 – 16

Thoughts ~ Insights

_____
_____
_____
_____
_____
_____
_____
_____
_____
_____

Titus
Stay True

Writer of Titus: Apostle Paul

Purpose of Titus: To encourage and give advice to Titus concerning opposition, instructions about good conduct and warnings about false teachers.

Date of the Writing of Titus: Around A.D. 64

Key Verse in Titus: "This is a trustworthy statement; and concerning these things I want you to speak confidently, so that those who have believed God will be careful to engage in good deeds. These things are good and profitable for men" (**Titus 3:8**).

Key Message in Titus: Encouragement to the believers to demonstrate the genuineness of their faith in good living. Paul's letter to Titus underscores the importance of authenticity in the lives of God's servants.

Original Recipient of Titus: Titus, a Greek; likely converted to Christ through Paul's ministry. He was Paul's special representative to the Island of Crete.

James
Genuine Faith Equals Authentic Behavior

Writer of James: James, Jesus' Brother; A Leader in the Jerusalem Church

Purpose of James: To encourage Christians who because of persecution were scattered throughout the then known world. James also encourages believers to not just have faith but to demonstrate their faith through good deeds and by authentic Christian behavior.

Date of the Writing of James: Probably around A.D. 49 before the Jerusalem Council held in A.D. 50.

Key Verse in James: "But someone may *well* say, 'You have faith and I have works; show me your faith without the works, and I will show you my faith by my works.'" (**James 2:18**).

Key Message in James: Genuine faith produces authentic deeds.

Original Recipients of James: First-century Jewish Christians living in Gentile communities outside Palestine (scattered because of persecution).

Genesis
Book of Beginnings

Writer of Genesis: Moses

Purpose of Genesis: To record God's creation of the world including the first man and woman. It reveals God's desire to create and set apart a people to have a faith relationship with Him.

Date of the Writing of Genesis: Approximately 1446 – 1406 B.C.

Key Verses in Genesis: "In the beginning God created the heavens and the earth" (**Genesis 1:1**).

"God created man in His own image, in the image of God He created him; male and female He created them" (**Genesis 1:27**).
"And I will make you a great nation, and I will bless you, and make your name great; And so you shall be a blessing; I will bless those who bless you, and the one who curses you I will curse. And in you all the families of the earth will be blessed. (**Genesis 12: 2-3**).

Key Message in Genesis: How "it" all began. A key phrase in Genesis: "This is the account . . ."

Original Recipients of Genesis: The people of Israel

Week 24

Day 1
  Psalm 119:89 – 128
  Proverbs 7
  II Kings 17 – 19

Day 2
  Psalm 119: 129 – 176
  Proverbs 8
  II Kings 20 – 25

Day 3
  Psalms 120 – 121
  Proverbs 9
  Titus 1 – 3

Day 4
  Psalm 122
  Proverbs 10
  James 1 – 3

Day 5
  Psalms 123 – 124
  Proverbs 11
  James 4 – 5

Day 6
  Psalms 125 – 126
  Proverbs 12
  Genesis 1 – 3

Day 7
  Psalms 127 – 128
  Proverbs 13
  Genesis 4 – 5

Thoughts ~ Insights

_____
_____
_____
_____
_____
_____
_____
_____
_____
_____

Week 25

Day 1
Psalms 129 – 130
Proverbs 14
Genesis 6 – 7

Day 2
Psalms 131 – 132
Proverbs 15
Genesis 8 – 10

Day 3
Psalms 133 – 134
Proverbs 16
Genesis 11 – 13

Day 4
Psalm 135
Proverbs 17
Genesis 14 – 15

Day 5
Psalms 136 – 137
Proverbs 18
Genesis 16 – 18

Day 6
Psalm 138
Proverbs 19
Genesis 19 – 20

Day 7
Psalm 139
Proverbs 20
Genesis 21 – 22

Thoughts ~ Insights

_____
_____
_____
_____
_____
_____
_____
_____
_____

Week 26

Day 1
Psalms 140 – 141
Proverbs 21
Genesis 23 – 24

Day 2
Psalms 142 – 143
Proverbs 22
Genesis 25 – 26

Day 3
Psalm 144
Proverbs 23
Genesis 27 – 28

Day 4
Psalms 145 – 146
Proverbs 24
Genesis 29 – 30

Day 5
Psalm 147
Proverbs 25
Genesis 31 – 32

Day 6
Psalms 148 – 149
Proverbs 26
Genesis 33 – 34

Day 7
Psalm 150
Proverbs 27
Genesis 35 – 36

Thoughts ~ Insights

_____
_____
_____
_____
_____
_____
_____
_____
_____
_____
_____

II Corinthians
A Man and His Ministry

Writer of II Corinthians: Apostle Paul

Purpose of II Corinthians: Paul affirms his calling, his ministry and defends his authority as an apostle. The letter is also written to refute and correct false teaching in the church in Corinth.

Date of the Writing of II Corinthians: About A.D. 55

Key Verse in II Corinthians: "Therefore, we are ambassadors for Christ, as though God were making an appeal through us; we beg you on behalf of Christ, be reconciled to God" (**II Corinthians 5:20**).

Key Message in II Corinthians: Written in defense of Paul's authority as an apostle and to denounce those who were twisting the truth.

Original Recipients of II Corinthians: The Church in Corinth.

Day 1
  Psalms 1 – 2
  Proverbs 28
  Genesis 37 – 39

Day 2
  Psalms 3 – 4
  Proverbs 29
  Genesis 40 – 42

Day 3
  Psalms 5 – 6
  Proverbs 30
  Genesis 43 – 45

Day 4
  Psalms 7 – 8
  Proverbs 31
  Genesis 46 – 48

Day 5
  Psalm 9
  Proverbs 1
  Genesis 49 – 50

Day 6
  Psalms 10 – 11
  Proverbs 2
  II Corinthians 1 – 3

Day 7
  Psalms 12 – 13
  Proverbs 3
  II Corinthians 4 – 6

Thoughts ~ Insights

_____
_____
_____
_____
_____
_____
_____
_____
_____
_____

Jonah
The Reluctant Prophet

Writer of Jonah: Jonah

Purpose of Jonah: To show the compassionate heart and grace of God—to offer the message of salvation to all, even to the enemies of His people.

Date of the Writing of Jonah: Around 785 – 750 B.C.

Key Verse in Jonah: "Should I not have compassion on Nineveh, the great city in which there are more than 120,000 persons who do not know *the difference* between their right and left hand, as well as many animals?" (**Jonah 4:11**).

Key Message in Jonah: To show the unmeasurable mercy and grace of God.

Original Recipients of Jonah: The People of Israel

Haggai
The Prophet of Action—Finish What has been Started

Writer of Haggai: Haggai; born in Babylonian captivity. His name means "festive."

Purpose of Haggai: To spur the post-captivity people of Judah to complete the re-building of the temple.

Date of the Writing of Haggai: About 520 B.C.

Key Verse in Haggai: "Is it time for you yourselves to dwell in your paneled houses while this house *lies* desolate?" (**Haggai 1:4**).

Key Message in Haggai: To complete the re-building of the Temple in Jerusalem.

Original Recipients of Haggai: The people living in the city of Jerusalem and those who had returned from exile.

Esther
The Woman of the Hour

Writer of Esther: Unknown

Purpose of Esther: The Book of Esther is unique in that the name of God is never mentioned and is never quoted or referred to in the New testament. But it does have a vital purpose in that it is a permanent record of the preservation of God's people during a very harsh time while in captivity under Persian rule.

Date of the Writing of Esther: Approximately 470 B.C.

Key Verse in Esther: "For if you remain silent at this time, relief and deliverance will arise for the Jews from another place and you and your father's house will perish. And who knows whether you have not attained royalty for such a time as this?" (**Esther 4:14**).

Key Message in Esther: To see God at work behind the scenes to preserve and protect His people when threatened by those who would destroy them.

Original Recipients of Esther: The People of Israel

Week 28

Day 1
  Psalms 14 – 15
  Proverbs 4
  II Corinthians 7 – 9

Day 2
  Psalm 16
  Proverbs 5
  II Corinthians 10 – 11

Day 3
  Psalm 17
  Proverbs 6
  II Corinthians 12 – 13

Day 4
  Psalm 18
  Proverbs 7
  Jonah 1 – 4

Day 5
  Psalms 19 – 20
  Proverbs 8
  Haggai 1 – 2

Day 6
  Psalm 21
  Proverbs 9
  Esther 1 – 3

Day 7
  Psalm 22
  Proverbs 10
  Esther 4 – 7

Thoughts ~ Insights

_____
_____
_____
_____
_____
_____
_____
_____
_____
_____

Mark
Jesus, the Suffering Servant

Writer of Mark: John Mark (likely received much of his information from Peter, the Apostle).

Purpose of Mark: Mark is believed to be the earliest of the four gospels and also the briefest. Mark approached the writing of the gospel with an almost breathless passion and sense of urgency to show a picture of a suffering servant with the power to heal and through His death and resurrection to bring life.

Date of Mark: Probably between A.D. 55 and 65

Key Verse in Mark: "For even the Son of Man did not come to be served, but to serve, and to give His life a ransom for many" (**Mark 10:45**).

Key Message in Mark: Jesus is the suffering servant who came to die so that all who believe in Him may have life everlasting.

Original Recipients of Mark: The Christians in Rome

Week 29

Day 1
  Psalms 23 – 24
  Proverbs 11
  Esther 8 – 10

Day 2
  Psalms 25 – 26
  Proverbs 12
  Mark 1 – 3

Day 3
  Psalms 27 – 28
  Proverbs 13
  Mark 4 – 5

Day 4
  Psalms 29 – 30
  Proverbs 14
  Mark 6 – 8

Day 5
  Psalms 31 – 32
  Proverbs 15
  Mark 9 – 10

Day 6
  Psalms 33 – 34
  Proverbs 16
  Mark 11 – 12

Day 7
  Psalm 35
  Proverbs 17
  Mark 13 – 14

Thoughts ~ Insights

_____
_____
_____
_____
_____
_____
_____
_____
_____
_____

Isaiah
Prince Among the Prophets

Writer of Isaiah: The Prophet Isaiah

Purpose of Isaiah: To call the people of Judah back to God, to warn of God's judgment if they did not return and to tell of God's provision of salvation through the coming of the promised Messiah.

Date of the Writing of Isaiah: About 700 B.C.

Key Verses in the Book of Isaiah: "He was despised and forsaken of men, a man of sorrows and acquainted with grief; And like one from whom men hide their face He was despised, and we did not esteem Him. Surely our griefs He Himself bore, and our sorrows He carried; Yet we ourselves esteemed Him stricken, smitten of God, and afflicted. But He was pierced through for our transgressions, He was crushed for our iniquities; The chastening for our well-being *fell* upon Him, and by His scourging we are healed" **(Isaiah 53:3-5)**.

Key Message in Isaiah: The Book of Isaiah portrays a beautiful portrait of the Messiah; some portions like in the 53rd chapter are remarkedly written in the past tense, 700 years before the incarnation of Christ.

Original Recipients of Isaiah: The people of the Southern Kingdom of Judah.

Week 30

Day 1
  Psalms 36 – 37
  Proverbs 18
  Mark 15 – 16

Day 2
  Psalms 38 – 39
  Proverbs 19
  Isaiah 1 – 4

Day 3
  Psalms 40 – 41
  Proverbs 20
  Isaiah 5 – 8

Day 4
  Psalms 42 – 43
  Proverbs 21
  Isaiah 9 – 12

Day 5
  Psalm 44
  Proverbs 22
  Isaiah 13- 16

Day 6
  Psalms 45 – 46
  Proverbs 23
  Isaiah 17 – 18

Day 7
  Psalms 47 – 48
  Proverbs 24
  Isaiah 19 – 20

Thoughts ~ Insights

_____
_____
_____
_____
_____
_____
_____
_____
_____
_____

Week 31

Day 1
Psalm 49
Proverbs 25
Isaiah 21 – 23

Day 2
Psalms 50
Proverbs 26
Isaiah 24 – 26

Day 3
Psalms 51 - 52
Proverbs 27
Isaiah 27 – 29

Day 4
Psalm 53 - 54
Proverbs 28
Isaiah 30 – 31

Day 5
Psalms 55
Proverbs 29
Isaiah 32 – 33

Day 6
Psalms 56 – 57
Proverbs 30
Isaiah 34 – 36

Day 7
Psalms 58 – 59
Proverbs 31
Isaiah 37 – 40

Thoughts ~ Insights

_____
_____
_____
_____
_____
_____
_____
_____
_____
_____

Day 1
  Psalms 60 – 61
  Proverbs 1
  Isaiah 41 – 44

Day 2
  Psalms 62 – 63
  Proverbs 2
  Isaiah 45 – 48

Day 3
  Psalms 64 – 65
  Proverbs 3
  Isaiah 49 – 52

Day 4
  Psalms 66 – 67
  Proverbs 4
  Isaiah 53 – 56

Day 5
  Psalm 68
  Proverbs 5
  Isaiah 57 – 58

Day 6
  Psalm 69
  Proverbs 6
  Isaiah 59 – 61

Day 7
  Psalms 70 – 72
  Proverbs 7
  Isaiah 62 – 63

Thoughts ~ Insights

_____
_____
_____
_____
_____
_____
_____
_____
_____
_____

Galatians
Freedom in Christ

Writer of Galatians: The Apostle Paul

Purpose of Galatians: To refute the legalistic Jews who were teaching that Gentile believers must obey the Jewish laws in order to be saved.

Date of the Writing of Galatians: Approximately A.D. 49 prior to the Jerusalem Council **(Acts 15)** in A.D. 50.

Key Verses in Galatians: "Nevertheless knowing that a man is not justified by the works of the Law but through faith in Christ Jesus, even we have believed in Christ Jesus, so that we may be justified by faith in Christ and not by the works of the Law; since by the works of the Law no flesh will be justified **(Galatians 2:16)**.

"It was for freedom that Christ set us free; therefore keep standing firm and do not be subject again to a yoke of slavery" (**Galatians 5:1**).

 Key Message in Galatians: We are justified by faith in Jesus Christ, not by works of the law.

Original Recipients of Galatians: The churches in southern Galatia, planted by Paul on his first missionary journey including Iconium, Lystra and Derbe.

Song of Solomon
A Poem of Celebrated Love

Writer of Song of Solomon: Solomon

Purpose of Song of Solomon: To beautifully portray the love between a bridegroom (King Solomon) and his bride, to affirm the sanctity of marriage and to picture God's love for His people.

Date of the Writing of Song of Solomon: Approximately 970 – 930 B.C.

Key Verse in Song of Solomon "I am my beloved's and my beloved is mine, He who pastures *his flock* among the lilies" (**Song of Solomon 6:3**).

Key Message in Song of Solomon: The joy and intimacy of love within a committed marriage relationship.

Original Recipients of the Song of Solomon: The people of Israel

Week 33

Day 1
 Psalms 73 – 74
 Proverbs 8
 Isaiah 64 – 66

Day 2
 Psalms 75 – 76
 Proverbs 9
 Galatians 1 – 2

Day 3
 Psalm 77
 Proverbs 10
 Galatians 3 – 4

Day 4
 Psalm 78
 Proverbs 11
 Galatians 5 – 6

Day 5
 Psalms 79 – 80
 Proverbs 12
 Song of Solomon 1 – 3

Day 6
 Psalms 81 – 82
 Proverbs 13
 Song of Solomon 4 – 6

Day 7
 Psalms 83 – 84
 Proverbs 14
 Song of Solomon 7 – 8

Thoughts ~ Insights

_____
_____
_____
_____
_____
_____
_____
_____
_____
_____

Exodus
The Story of a Miraculous Deliverance

Writer of Exodus: Moses

Purpose of Exodus: To record the events of Israel's deliverance from Egyptian bondage, their development as a nation and their receiving of the law from God.

Date of the Writing of Exodus: Around 1440 B.C.

Key Verses in Exodus: "The LORD said, 'I have surely seen the affliction of My people who are in Egypt, and have given heed to their cry because of their taskmasters, for I am aware of their sufferings. So I have come down to deliver them from the power of the Egyptians, and to bring them up from that land to a good and spacious land, to a land flowing with milk and honey . . . Therefore, come now, and I will send you to Pharaoh, so that you may bring My people, the sons of Israel, out of Egypt'" (**Exodus 3:7-10**).

Key Message in Exodus: The story of how God delivered His people from 400 years of bondage.

Original Recipients of Exodus: The People of Israel

Week 34

Day 1
Psalms 85 – 86
Proverbs 15
Exodus 1 – 3

Day 2
Psalms 87 – 88
Proverbs 16
Exodus 4 – 7

Day 3
Psalm 89
Proverbs 17
Exodus 8 – 10

Day 4
Psalms 90 – 92
Proverbs 18
Exodus 11 – 13

Day 5
Psalms 93 – 94
Proverbs 19
Exodus 14 – 15

Day 6
Psalms 95 - 96
Proverbs 20
Exodus 16 – 18

Day 7
Psalms 97 – 98
Proverbs 21
Exodus 19 – 20

Thoughts ~ Insights

_____
_____
_____
_____
_____
_____
_____
_____
_____
_____

Week 35

Day 1
   Psalms 99 – 101
   Proverbs 22
   Exodus 21 – 22

Day 2
   Psalms 102 – 103
   Proverbs 23
   Exodus 23 – 25

Day 3
   Psalm 104
   Proverbs 24
   Exodus 26 – 28

Day 4
   Psalm 105
   Proverbs 25
   Exodus 29 – 31

Day 5
   Psalm 106
   Proverbs 26
   Exodus 32 – 34

Day 6
   Psalm 107
   Proverbs 27
   Exodus 35 – 37

Day 7
   Psalms 108 – 109
   Proverbs 28
   Exodus 38 – 40

Thoughts ~ Insights

_____
_____
_____
_____
_____
_____
_____
_____
_____
_____

Acts
Birth and Acts of the Early Church

Writer of Acts: Luke, A Gentile Physician

Purpose of Acts: To record the events after the resurrection of Jesus and the birth and growth of the Church.

Date of the Writing of Acts: Between A.D. 63 and 70

Key Verse in Acts: "He (Jesus) said to them, 'It is not for you to know times or epochs which the Father has fixed by His own authority; but you will receive power when the Holy Spirit has come upon you; and you shall be My witnesses both in Jerusalem, and in all Judea and Samaria, and even to the remotest part of the earth'" (**Acts 1:7-8**).

Key Message in Acts: To give an account of the growth, outreach and global impact of the early church.

Original Recipient of Acts: Theophilus

Day 1
  Psalms 110 – 111
  Proverbs 29
  Acts 1 – 3

Day 2
  Psalms 112 – 113
  Proverbs 30
  Acts 4 – 6

Day 3
  Psalms 114 – 115
  Proverbs 31
  Acts 7 – 9

Day 4
  Psalms 116 – 117
  Proverbs 1
  Acts 10 – 12

Day 5
  Psalm 118
  Proverbs 2
  Acts 13 – 15

Day 6
  Psalm 119:1 – 48
  Provers 3
  Acts 16 – 18

Day 7
  Psalm 119:49 – 88
  Proverbs 4
  Acts 19 – 21

Thoughts ~ Insights

_____
_____
_____
_____
_____
_____
_____
_____
_____
_____

Habakkuk
Watchman on the Wall

Writer of Habakkuk: The Prophet Habakkuk

Purpose of Habakkuk: To show, even at evil times that God is still in control and that God does not allow evil to endure forever.

Date of the Writing of Habakkuk: Somewhere around 610 – 588 B.C.

Key Verses in Habakkuk: "I will stand on my guard post and station myself on the rampart; And I will keep watch to see what He will speak to me . . . Then the LORD answered me and said, 'Record the vision and inscribe *it* on tablets . . . For the vision is yet for the appointed time; It hastens toward the goal and it will not fail. Though it tarries, wait for it; for it will certainly come, it will not delay. Behold, as for the proud one, his soul is not right within him; But the righteous will live by his faith'" (**Habakkuk 2:1-4**).

Key Message in Habakkuk: God never abandons His people even during evil and desperate times.

Original Recipients of Habakkuk: The Southern Kingdom of Judah

Malachi
God's Last Spokesman Before the Silent Years

Writer of Malachi: The Prophet Malachi

Purpose of Malachi: To confront God's People with their sins and apathetic complacency and urge them to return to Him.

Date of the Writing of Malachi: Approximately 430 B.C.

Key Verse in Malachi: "From the days of your fathers you have turned aside from My statutes and have not kept *them*. Return to Me, and I will return to you," says the LORD of hosts" (**Malachi 3:7**).

Key Message in Malachi: Malachi confronted the deplorable conditions that he saw in his day: spiritual indifference, intermarriage with foreigners, neglect of the tithe and offerings of blemished sacrifices. After Malachi, God would not speak again for 400 years.

Original Recipients of Malachi: The people in Jerusalem

I Chronicles
A Narrative of Israel's History

Writer of I Chronicles: Ezra, According to Jewish Tradition

Purpose of I Chronicles: To trace the roots of the nation of Israel beginning with Adam and generations that followed. It also records the reign of David as the king of Israel.

Date of the Writing of I Chronicles: Between 450 – 400 B.C.

Key Verse in I Chronicles: "And David realized that the LORD had established him as king over Israel, *and* that his kingdom was highly exalted, for the sake of His people Israel" **(I Chronicles 14:2**).

Key Message in I Chronicles: To encourage God's people to recognize their roots and to rediscover their God-ordained heritage.

Original Recipients of I Chronicles: The Exiles who returned from Captivity

Week 37

Day 1
  Psalm 119:89 – 128
  Proverbs 5
  Acts 22 – 24

Day 2
  Psalm 119: 129 – 176
  Proverbs 6
  Acts 25 – 26

Day 3
  Psalms 120 – 121
  Proverbs 7
  Acts 27 – 28

Day 4
  Psalm 122
  Proverbs 8
  Habakkuk 1 – 3

Day 5
  Psalms 123 – 124
  Proverbs 9
  Malachi 1 – 2

Day 6
  Psalms 125 – 126
  Proverbs 10
  Malachi 3 – 4

Day 7
  Psalms 127 – 128
  Proverbs 11
  I Chronicles 1 – 5

Thoughts ~ Insights

_____
_____
_____
_____
_____
_____
_____
_____
_____
_____

Week 38

Day 1
Psalms 129 – 130
Proverbs 12
I Chronicles 6 – 9

Day 2
Psalms 131 – 132
Proverbs 13
I Chronicles 10 – 12

Day 3
Psalms 133 – 134
Proverbs 14
I Chronicles 13 – 15

Day 4
Psalm 135
Proverbs 15
I Chronicles 16 – 18

Day 5
Psalms 136 – 137
Proverbs 16
I Chronicles 19 – 21

Day 6
Psalm 138
Proverbs 17
I Chronicles 22 – 24

Day 7
Psalm 139
Proverbs 18
I Chronicles 25 – 27

Thoughts ~ Insights

_____
_____
_____
_____
_____
_____
_____
_____
_____
_____

II Chronicles
Demise of the Nations of Israel and Judah

Writer of II Chronicles: Ezra, According to Jewish Tradition

Purpose of II Chronicles: To make a record of the Kings of Judah and Israel, both the good and the bad and to encourage the nations of Israel and Judah to obedience toward God and His law.

Date of the Writing of II Chronicles: Between 450 – 400 B.C.

Key Verse in II Chronicles: "If My people who are called by My name humble themselves and pray and seek My face and turn from their wicked ways, then I will hear from heaven, will forgive their sin and will heal their land" (**II Chronicles 7:14**).

Key Message in II Chronicles: A powerful reminder that a nation and a people who will honor God will see wonderful success. Those who will not honor God and turn from Him will experience a great downfall.

Original Recipients of II Chronicles: The exiles who returned from captivity

Week 39

Day 1
  Psalms 140 – 141
  Proverbs 19
  I Chronicles 28 – 29

Day 2
  Psalms 142 – 143
  Proverbs 20
  II Chronicles 1 – 4

Day 3
  Psalm 144
  Proverbs 21
  II Chronicles 5 – 6

Day 4
  Psalms 145 – 146
  Proverbs 22
  II Chronicles 7 – 8

Day 5
  Psalm 147
  Proverbs 23
  II Chronicles 9 – 11

Day 6
  Psalms 148 – 149
  Proverbs 24
  II Chronicles 12 – 14

Day 7
  Psalm 150
  Proverbs 25
  II Chronicles 15 – 17

Thoughts ~ Insights

_____
_____
_____
_____
_____
_____
_____
_____
_____
_____

Hebrews
Meet Our Redeemer Priest

Writer of Hebrews: Unknown

Purpose of Hebrews: To present the superiority and sufficiency of Christ as High Priest and to encourage believers not to fall away from the faith.

Date of the Writing of Hebrews: Possibly A.D. 70

Key Verse in Hebrews: "And He (Jesus) is the radiance of His glory and the exact representation of His nature, and upholds all things by the word of His power. When He had made purification of sins, He sat down at the right hand of the Majesty on high" (**Hebrews 1:3**).

Key Message in Hebrews: To set forth the absolute superiority of Christ.

Original Recipients of Hebrews: Hebrew Christians

Week 40

Day 1
  Psalms 1 – 2
  Proverbs 26
  II Chronicles 18 – 19

Day 2
  Psalms 3 – 4
  Proverbs 27
  II Chronicles 20 – 23

Day 3
  Psalms 5 – 6
  Proverbs 28
  II Chronicles 24 – 26

Day 4
  Psalms 7 – 8
  Proverbs 29
  II Chronicles 27 – 29

Day 5
  Psalm 9
  Proverbs 30
  II Chronicles 30 – 33

Day 6
  Psalms 10 – 11
  Proverbs 31
  II Chronicles 34 – 36

Day 7
  Psalms 12 – 13
  Proverbs 1
  Hebrews 1 – 3

Thoughts ~ Insights

_____
_____
_____
_____
_____
_____
_____
_____
_____
_____

Job
Why do the Righteous Suffer?

Writer of Job: Unknown

Purpose of Job: To illustrate God's supreme sovereignty and to demonstrate true faith even in the midst of suffering and trouble.

Date of the Writing of Job: Unknown; possibly during the time of the Patriarchs, approximately 2000 – 1800 B.C. Many scholars believe that Job was the first book of the Bible to be written.

Key Verse in Job: "The LORD said to Satan, 'Have you considered My servant Job? For there is no one like him on the earth, a blameless and upright man fearing God and turning away from evil. And he still holds fast his integrity, although you incited Me against him to ruin him without cause'" (**Job 2:3**).

Key Message in Job: Deals with the mystery of suffering—Why do the good and righteous suffer?

Original Recipients of Job: Unknown. Ezekiel (14:14) and James (5:11) both mention Job as a historical character.

Week 41

Day 1
 Psalms 14 – 15
 Proverbs 2
 Hebrews 4 – 6

Day 2
 Psalm 16
 Proverbs 3
 Hebrews 7 – 9

Day 3
 Psalm 17
 Proverbs 4
 Hebrews 10 – 11

Day 4
 Psalm 18
 Proverbs 5
 Hebrews 12 – 13

Day 5
 Psalms 19 – 20
 Proverbs 6
 Job 1 – 3

Day 6
 Psalm 21
 Proverbs 7
 Job 4 – 6

Day 7
 Psalm 22
 Proverbs 8
 Job 7 – 9

Thoughts ~ Insights

_____
_____
_____
_____
_____
_____
_____
_____
_____

Week 42

Day 1
  Psalms 23 – 24
  Proverbs 9
  Job 10 – 12

Day 2
  Psalms 25 – 26
  Proverbs 10
  Job 13 – 15

Day 3
  Psalms 27 – 28
  Proverbs 11
  Job 16 – 18

Day 4
  Psalms 29 – 30
  Proverbs 12
  Job 19 – 21

Day 5
  Psalms 31 – 32
  Proverbs 13
  Job 22 – 24

Day 6
  Psalms 33 – 34
  Proverbs 14
  Job 25 – 27

Day 7
  Psalm 35
  Proverbs 15
  Job 28 – 30

Thoughts ~ Insights

_____
_____
_____
_____
_____
_____
_____
_____
_____

I Thessalonians
A Practical and Personal Letter

Writer of I Thessalonians: The Apostle Paul; believed to be the first letter Paul wrote that found its way into the New Testament.

Purpose of I Thessalonians: To encourage and strengthen the Thessalonian Christians in their trials of faith and to give them assurance of Christ's return.

Date of the Writing of I Thessalonians: About A.D. 50-51

Key Verse in I Thessalonians: "For if we believe that Jesus died and rose again, even so God will bring with Him those who have fallen asleep in Jesus" (**I Thessalonians 4:14**).

Key Message in I Thessalonians: The revealing of a pastor's (the Apostle Paul) heart to a group of young believers who are growing together and facing opposition. In the letter, Paul also answers some crucial questions, particularly concerning the return of our Lord.

Original Recipients of I Thessalonians: The Church at Thessalonica

Week 43

Day 1
  Psalms 36 – 37
  Proverbs 16
  Job 31 – 33

Day 2
  Psalms 38 – 39
  Proverbs 17
  Job 34 – 36

Day 3
  Psalms 40 – 41
  Proverbs 18
  Job 37 – 38

Day 4
  Psalms 42 – 43
  Proverbs 19
  Job 39 – 40

Day 5
  Psalm 44
  Proverbs 20
  Job 41 – 42

Day 6
  Psalms 45 – 46
  Proverbs 21
  I Thessalonians 1 – 3

Day 7
  Psalms 47 – 48
  Proverbs 22
  I Thessalonians 4 – 5

Thoughts ~ Insights

_____
_____
_____
_____
_____
_____
_____
_____
_____
_____

II Thessalonians
About the Lord's Return

Writer of II Thessalonians: The Apostle Paul

Purpose of II Thessalonians: To encourage the Church in Thessalonica to stand firm in the faith and to clear up confusion and misunderstanding about the Lord's return among the Christians in Thessalonica.

Date of the Writing of II Thessalonians: Approximately A.D. 51 or 52

Key Verse in II Thessalonians: "So then, brethren, stand firm and hold to the traditions which you were taught, whether by word *of mouth* or by letter from us" (**II Thessalonians 2:15**).

Key Message in II Thessalonians: To encourage the Christians in Thessalonica, as they wait for the Lord's return to be alert, aware of deceptive forces surrounding them, and to remain confident in God's plan.

Original Recipients of II Thessalonians: The Church in Thessalonica

Jude
Defender of the Faith

Writer of Jude: Jude, brother of Jesus and James

Purpose of Jude: To encourage believers to stand strong in the faith, defend the Gospel and to oppose false teachers and false teaching.

Date of the Writing of Jude: Around A.D. 65

Key Verse in Letter of Jude: "Beloved, while I was making every effort to write you about our common salvation, I felt the necessity to write to you appealing that you contend earnestly for the faith which was once for all handed down to the saints" (**Verse 3**).

Key Message in Jude: To defend the apostolic faith and to encourage believers to do the same.

Original Recipients of Jude: Jewish Christians

Leviticus
Guidebook for Holy Living

Writer of Leviticus: Moses

Purpose of Leviticus: Directions for the Priests and Levites to properly lead the People of Israel to worship a Holy God. It also serves as God's directions for the people of Israel to live separate and holy lives. The most significant word in the Book of Leviticus is the word, "holy." It occurs 74 times.

Date of the Writing of Leviticus: About 1440 B.C.

Key Verse in Leviticus: "Speak to all the congregation of the sons of Israel and say to them, 'You shall be holy, for I the LORD your God am holy'" (**Leviticus 19:2**).

Key Message in Leviticus: To help unholy and sinful people learn how to worship and serve a holy God.

Original Recipients of Leviticus: The People of Israel

Week 44

Day 1
Psalm 49
Proverbs 23
II Thessalonians 1 – 3

Day 2
Psalm 50
Proverbs 24
Jude

Day 3
Psalms 51 – 52
Proverbs 25
Leviticus 1 – 2

Day 4
Psalms 53 – 54
Proverbs 26
Leviticus 3 – 4

Day 5
Psalm 55
Proverbs 27
Leviticus 5 – 6

Day 6
Psalms 56 – 57
Proverbs 28
Leviticus 7 – 9

Day 7
Psalms 58 – 59
Proverbs 29
Leviticus 10 – 12

Thoughts ~ Insights

_____
_____
_____
_____
_____
_____
_____
_____
_____
_____

I Peter
Encouragement for Suffering Christians

Writer of I Peter: The Apostle Peter

Purpose of I Peter: To give hope and encouragement to scattered and suffering Christians.

Date of the Writing of I Peter: Between A.D. 60 – 64

Key Verses in I Peter: "In this you greatly rejoice, even though now for a little while, if necessary, you have been distressed by various trials, so that the proof of your faith, *being* more precious than gold which is perishable, even though tested by fire, may be found to result in praise and glory and honor at the revelation of Jesus Christ: (**I Peter 1:6-7**).

Key Message in I Peter: Encouragement to endure suffering and to stand fast in the grace and sufficiency of God.

Original Recipients of I Peter: Jewish Christians who because of persecution had been scattered throughout Asia Minor.

Week 45

Day 1
  Psalms 60 – 61
  Proverbs 30
  Leviticus 13 – 15

Day 2
  Psalms 62 – 63
  Proverbs 31
  Leviticus 16 – 18

Day 3
  Psalm 64 – 65
  Proverbs 1
  Leviticus 19 – 20

Day 4
  Psalm 66 – 67
  Proverbs 2
  Leviticus 21 – 22

Day 5
  Psalms 68
  Proverbs 3
  Leviticus 23 – 24

Day 6
  Psalm 69
  Proverbs 4
  Leviticus 25 – 27

Day 7 Psalm 70 – 72
  Proverbs 5
  I Peter 1 – 3

Thoughts ~ Insights

_____
_____
_____
_____
_____
_____
_____
_____
_____

II Peter
Be Alert . . . Be Watchful

Writer of II Peter: The Apostle Peter

Purpose of II Peter: To Warn against false teaching and doctrinal error in the last days and in view of the Lord's return.

Date of the Writing of II Peter: Possibly around A.D. 67

Key Verses in II Peter: "Grace and peace be multiplied to you in the knowledge of God and of Jesus our Lord; seeing that His divine power has granted to us everything pertaining to life and godliness, through the true knowledge of Him who called us by His own glory and excellence" (**II Peter 1:2-3**).

Key Message in II Peter: Peter encourages believers to live a life of service and purity as they await the Lord's return.

Original Recipients of II Peter: The Church at Large

Hosea
Unfaithfulness

Writer of Hosea: Hosea

Purpose of Hosea: To illustrate God's love and compassion for His people even though they have broken their covenant relationship and are unfaithful to Him.

Date of the Writing of Hosea: Approximately 715 B.C.

Key Verse in the Book of Hosea: "Then the LORD said to me, 'Go again, love a woman *who* is loved by *her* husband, yet an adulteress, even as the LORD loves the sons of Israel, though they turn to other gods and love raisin cakes'" (**Hosea 3:1**).

Key Message in Hosea: God's love for His people, even when they are unfaithful to Him.

Original Recipients of Hosea: The People of the Northern Kingdom of Israel

Week 46

Day 1
  Psalms 73 – 74
  Proverbs 6
  I Peter 4 – 5

Day 2
  Psalms 75 – 76
  Proverbs 7
  II Peter 1 – 3

Day 3
  Psalm 77
  Proverbs 8
  Hosea 1 – 2

Day 4
  Psalm 78
  Proverbs 9
  Hosea 3 – 4

Day 5
  Psalms 79 – 80
  Proverbs 10
  Hosea 5 – 6

Day 6
  Psalms 81 – 82
  Proverbs 11
  Hosea 7 – 8

Day 7
  Psalms 83 – 84
  Proverbs 12
  Hosea 9 – 10

Thoughts ~ Insights

_____
_____
_____
_____
_____
_____
_____
_____
_____
_____

Ezekiel
The Street Preacher

Writer of Ezekiel: Ezekiel

Purpose of Ezekiel: To announce in a clear and illustrative way God's judgement on Israel and other disobedient nations and to foretell the eventual salvation of God's people.

Date of the Writing of Ezekiel: Approximately 571 B.C.

Key Verses in Ezekiel: "For I will take you from the nations, gather you from all the lands and bring you into your own land. Then I will sprinkle clean water on you, and you will be clean; I will cleanse you from all your filthiness and from all your idols. Moreover, I will give you a new heart and put a new spirit within you; and I will remove the heart of stone from your flesh and give you a heart of flesh" (**Ezekiel 36:24-26**).

Key Message in Ezekiel: Our hope is in God alone.

Original Recipients of Ezekiel: The Jewish People in captivity in Babylonian.

Week 47

Day 1
  Psalms 85 – 86
  Proverbs 13
  Hosea 11 – 12

Day 2
  Psalms 87 – 88
  Proverbs 14
  Hosea 13 – 14

Day 3
  Psalm 89
  Proverbs 15
  Ezekiel 1 – 2

Day 4
  Psalms 90 – 92
  Proverbs 16
  Ezekiel 3 – 4

Day 5
  Psalms 93 – 94
  Proverbs 17
  Ezekiel 5 – 6

Day 6
  Psalms 95 – 96
  Proverbs 18
  Ezekiel 7 – 8

Day 7
  Psalms 97 – 98
  Proverbs 19
  Ezekiel 9 – 11

Thoughts ~ Insights

_____
_____
_____
_____
_____
_____
_____
_____
_____

Week 48

Day 1
  Psalms 99 – 101
  Proverbs 20
  Ezekiel 12 – 13

Day 2
  Psalms 102 – 103
  Proverbs 21
  Ezekiel 14 – 16

Day 3
  Psalms 104
  Proverbs 22
  Ezekiel 17 – 18

Day 4
  Psalm 105
  Proverbs 23
  Ezekiel 19 – 21

Day 5
  Psalm 106
  Proverbs 24
  Ezekiel 22 – 23

Day 6
  Psalm 107
  Proverbs 25
  Ezekiel 24 – 25

Day 7
  Psalms 108 – 109
  Proverbs 26
  Ezekiel 26 – 27

Thoughts ~ Insights

_____
_____
_____
_____
_____
_____
_____
_____
_____
_____

Week 49

Day 1
  Psalms 110 – 111
  Proverbs 27
  Ezekiel 28 – 29

Day 2
  Psalms 112 – 113
  Proverbs 28
  Ezekiel 30 – 31

Day 3
  Psalms 114 – 115
  Proverbs 29
  Ezekiel 32 – 33

Day 4
  Psalms 116 – 117
  Proverbs 30
  Ezekiel 34 – 35

Day 5
  Psalm 118
  Proverbs 31
  Ezekiel 36 – 38

Day 6
  Psalm 119:1 – 48
  Proverbs 1
  Ezekiel 39 – 40

Day 7
  Psalm 119:49 – 88
  Proverbs 2
  Ezekiel 41 – 42

Thoughts ~ Insights

_____
_____
_____
_____
_____
_____
_____
_____
_____
_____

II John
Letter to a Lady and Her Children

Writer of II John: John the Apostle

Purpose of II John: To warn against false teachers—those who do not teach the truth about Jesus.

Date of the writing of II John: Probably A.D. 90, written from Ephesus.

Key Verse in II John: "And this is love, that we walk according to His commandments. This is the commandment, just as you have heard from the beginning, that you should walk in it" (**Verse 6**).

Key Message in II John: John urges this "chosen lady and her children" to continue to walk in truth and in love and to stand against error.

Original Recipients of II John: To the "chosen lady" and her children—or possibly to a local church.

III John
Three Men

Writer of III John: The Apostle John

Purpose of III John: To demonstrate three different types of people in the church by examining the actions of three actual men in the early church: Gaius, Diotrephes and Demetrius.

Date of the Writing of III John: Between A.D. 85 – 95 from Ephesus

Key Verse in III John: "Beloved (Gaius), you are acting faithfully in whatever you accomplish for the brethren, and especially *when they are* strangers" (**Verse 5**).

Key Message in III John: Correct doctrine must be reflected in correct and practical behavior.

Original Recipient of III John: Gaius, A faithful Christian.

Nehemiah
Rebuilding Broken Walls

Writer of Nehemiah: Possibly Nehemiah with the aid of Ezra.

Purpose of Nehemiah: The last of the historical books in the Old Testament, the Book of Nehemiah records the third return of the exiles from captivity and the rebuilding of the wall around Jerusalem.

Date of the Writing of Nehemiah: Probably Around 430 B.C.

Key Verses in Nehemiah: "So the wall was completed on the twenty-fifth of *the month* Elul, in fifty-two days. When all our enemies heard *of it,* and all the nations surrounding us saw *it,* they lost their confidence; for they recognized that this work had been accomplished with the help of our God" (**Nehemiah 6:15-16**).

Key Message in Nehemiah: The right man at the right time for the right job: To direct the people in Jerusalem to rebuild the wall around the city and to restore their spiritual heritage.

Original Recipients of Nehemiah: The returning exiles from captivity.

Week 50

Day 1
　Psalm 119: 89 – 128
　Proverbs 3
　Ezekiel 43 – 44

Day 2
　Psalm 119:129 – 176
　Proverbs 4
　Ezekiel 45 – 46

Day 3
　Psalms 120 – 121
　Proverbs 5
　Ezekiel 47 – 48

Day 4
　Psalm 122
　Proverbs 6
　II & III John

Day 5
　Psalms 123 – 124
　Proverbs 7
　Nehemiah 1 – 2

Day 6
　Psalms 125 – 126
　Proverbs 8
　Nehemiah 3 – 4

Day 7
　Psalms 127 – 128
　Proverbs 9
　Nehemiah 5 – 6

Thoughts ~ Insights

_____

_____

_____

_____

_____

_____

_____

_____

_____

Joel
Warning!

Writer of Joel: Joel

Purpose of Joel: To warn Judah of coming judgment because of their sins of complacency, self-centeredness and idolatry and to turn back to God.

Date of the writing of Joel: Approximately 835 B.C.

Key Verses in Joel: "Yet even now," declares the LORD, 'Return to Me with all your heart, and with fasting, weeping and mourning; and rend your heart and not your garments.' Now return to the LORD your God, for He is gracious and compassionate, slow to anger, abounding in lovingkindness and relenting of evil" **(Joel 2:12-13)**.

Key Message in Joel: Repentance must precede intimacy with God.

Original Recipients of Joel: The Southern Kingdom of Judah.

Matthew
The King and His Kingdom

Writer of Matthew: Matthew

Purpose of Matthew: To offer proof that Jesus Christ is the long-promised Messiah, the Eternal King who fulfilled Old Testament Scriptures.

Date of the Writing of Matthew: Approximately A.D. 70

Key Verse in Matthew: "Do not think that I came to abolish the Law or the Prophets; I did not come to abolish but to fulfill" **(Matthew 5:17).**

Key Message in Mathew: The Promised Messiah has come.

Original Recipients of Matthew: The Jewish People in Particular.

Week 51

Day 1
Psalms 129 – 130
Proverbs 10
Nehemiah 7 – 9

Day 2
Psalms 131 – 132
Proverbs 11
Nehemiah 10 – 11

Day 3
Psalms 133 – 134
Proverbs 12
Nehemiah 12 – 13

Day 4
Psalm 135
Proverbs 13
Joel 1 – 3

Day 5
Psalms 136 – 137
Proverbs 14
Matthew 1 – 3

Day 6
Psalm 138
Proverbs 15
Matthew 4 – 5

Day 7
Psalm 139
Proverbs 16
Matthew 6 – 7

Thoughts ~ Insights

_____
_____
_____
_____
_____
_____
_____
_____
_____
_____

Week 52

Day 1
  Psalms 140 – 141
  Proverbs 17
  Matthew 8 – 10

Day 2
  Psalms 142 – 143
  Proverbs 18
  Matthew 11 – 13

Day 3
  Psalm 144
  Proverbs 19
  Matthew 14 – 16

Day 4
  Psalms 145 – 146
  Proverbs 20
  Matthew 17 – 19

Day 5
  Psalm 147
  Proverbs 21
  Matthew 20 – 22

Day 6
  Psalms 148 – 149
  Proverbs 22
  Matthew 23 – 25

Day 7
  Psalm 150
  Proverbs 23
  Matthew 26 – 28

Thoughts ~ Insights

_____
_____
_____
_____
_____
_____
_____
_____
_____
_____

About the Author

Pastor Mel Hooten has 45 years' experience in Christian ministry. Since retiring from serving as a traditional church pastor in 2008, God has led him back to his roots to carry the gospel of Jesus Christ into the world of ranchers, rodeo riders, cowboys and cowgirls who often do not feel comfortable in traditional church. Folks who love western heritage, country music, working with livestock, or cowboys at heart who prefer a simple down-to-earth approach to life; these are those to whom Mel seeks out.

Pastor Mel has served as a church planter for the Western Heritage division of Texas Baptists to start the Cowboy Church of Tarrant County near Fort Worth, Texas. Currently Mel wants to continue to bring good news to those who seek the truth and make available his Bible messages, devotionals, and lessons for those who preach and teach.

Mel brings a simple gospel message with a western flair. In addition, God uses him to teach practical ways to ride the range with Jesus every day. The trails of life will bring us to rivers that must be crossed and steep hills we can't climb alone. With Jesus, we can weather the storms and ride through the valleys. He will give guidance and provisions when we get bucked off. Indeed, there is a trail that leads home. Mel's mission is to help every person he encounters to find it.

Mel and his wife, Karen, currently live in Aubrey, Texas. They like to travel in their RV and enjoy time with their grandchildren. They are available for ministry wherever God leads them.

Other Books by this Author

"The Gospel of John Cowboy Style, A Paraphrase of the Gospel of John in Cowboy Language"

"Searching Heart & Scripture with The Gospel of John Cowboy Style"

"Riding the Range with Jesus: A Collection of Cowboy Sermons with a Western Flair for the Cowboy and Country Preacher or Teacher"

Books may be ordered from <u>www.Amazon.com</u> or <u>www.barnesandnoble.com</u>

All scriptures are taken from the *New American Standard Bible* unless otherwise noted.

Made in the USA
Columbia, SC
01 May 2020